MICKEY'S
QUESTION and ANSWER
BOOK

by Ronnie Krauss

Publishers · GROSSET & DUNLAP · New York
A FILMWAYS COMPANY

BY THE SEA

Why is the ocean salty?

There is a lot of salt in the rocks and soil that make up the earth. When it rains, the water soaks into the ground and splashes over the rocks, taking the salt out of them. This salt-soaked water flows into rivers and, eventually, into the sea. For a very long time—millions of years!—this has been happening. Enough salt has been emptied into the oceans by now to keep them very salty.

Special thanks to Anita and Robin

Library of Congress Catalog Card No. 79-50667
ISBN: 0-448-16565-1 (Trade Edition)
ISBN: 0-448-13128-5 (Library Edition)
Copyright © MCMLXXIX Walt Disney Productions.
World Wide Rights Reserved
Printed in the United States of America.
Published simultaneously in Canada.

Where does sand come from?

For hundreds of thousands of years, rains and rivers have washed down mountains and over the land, bringing rocks down to the sea where they get broken up into very tiny bits and pieces. The minerals from the rocks (like salt, but there are others, too) wash out and continue on into the sea. The heavier pieces, or sand, stay on the beach.

What color is the ocean?

Oceans are different colors, but most are blue. This is because water does not have a color of its own, but reflects the color of the sky above—unless something else, like the plants and animals living in it, change it to another color. In very cold oceans, for example, there are certain types of tiny green creatures that make the water look green. In the Red Sea, tiny red creatures make the water look red.

When the sky above a blue sea gets cloudy, the water seems to turn gray and dark, too. Watch the ocean the next time you are there. Doesn't it change color when a cloud passes overhead?

What are tides?

Every day at the ocean, the water moves up on the shore and then moves down again. These up-and-down motions are called tides—high tide when the water reaches the highest point on the beach, and low tide when it goes down as far as it can. Tides are caused by a force in the moon that makes it pull on the earth, tugging hardest at the part of the earth closest to it. It is easy for water, since it is light and flows freely, to feel the moon's pull and to go up and down on the shore with it.

What is a wave?

A wave is a swell of water that forms when the wind breezes over the surface of the water, making it ripple. The stronger the wind, the more the water will ripple and the bigger the wave will be. Waves actually move up and down, although they look like they are going to and fro.

Where do seashells come from?

Seashells are the cast-off homes of sea animals called mollusks. Some common mollusks that you might know are snails and scallops. Mollusks have very soft bodies, so they need to wear hard outer-shells for protection.

What is seaweed?

Seaweed is a type of plant that lives in the sea. Like all green plants, seaweed uses the sun's energy to make food for itself—it combines sunlight with the chemicals in the salt water. Some seaweeds are the biggest plants in the world. One giant seaweed is called *macrocystis;* it grows up to 80 feet long and 600 feet wide!

Do other plants grow under water?

Yes, many plants grow under water. As long as they can get sunlight they can live, and the sun shines down about 600 feet in the water. In the ocean most plants are algae, which have none of the roots, leaves, flowers or seeds that land plants do. In ponds, some plants have roots and leaves that grow under water, and others, like water lilies, float on the top of the pond.

How does a pearl get inside an oyster?

The oysters actually make the pearls themselves. If a grain of sand gets inside the oyster's shell, it scratches the soft body of the oyster. To stop the sand grain from scratching, the oyster covers it with the same shiny material it uses to coat the inside of its shell. As layers gather around the sand, a round pearl is formed.

How do fish breathe under water?

Fish need oxygen in order to live, and they have special breathing slits in their bodies, called gills, that can take oxygen from water. The fish brings water into its mouth and passes it over the gills. The oxygen is taken out then, and the water goes out tiny holes in the side of the fish's head.

6

Can fish live out of water?

Fish can't live out of water for too long, although some fish can stay alive out of water for a few hours. It depends on their gills—the longer the gills can stay wet from having been in the water, the better off the fish will be if it must stay outside its lake or pond or sea home.

Do fish sleep?

Yes, most fish sleep, and the ones that don't completely fall asleep take naps. Because fish do not have protected places to sleep, they can't sleep too soundly—it just wouldn't be safe. Fish that live in lakes, rivers and ponds often sleep on or near the bottom, and some fish spend the entire winter snoozing there in the mud. You may have seen a fish sleep without knowing it because its eyes were open—but fish have no eyelids!

What's a school of fish?

A school of fish is a group of the same type of fish that swims and stays together. Fish swim in schools for protection, since the more fish there are in one bunch, the less chance they each have of being bullied by bigger fish. As a group, they might be bigger than some of the REALLY big fish that would like to nibble on them. Schools can be 25 fish or millions of fish. Some fish that live in schools are tuna, herring and smelt. Sharks, flounder and eels are fish that swim alone.

What's the biggest fish in the world? The smallest?

The whale shark is the biggest fish. It can be as long as 60 feet and weigh up to 15 tons (that's 30,000 pounds!) The smallest fish in the world is the goby. It's only 1/3 of an inch big!

How big are sharks?

There are many different kinds of sharks —about 300 of them. They are of different size. The biggest is the whale shark, and the smallest is the spiny dogfish shark, which is only about 4 feet long.

Are all sharks dangerous?

No, most sharks won't bother people at all (only about 25 of the 300 different kinds of sharks will), and most of the dangerous sharks live in the warm waters near the equator. The meanest and most ferocious—and probably the only shark that will attack and eat man —is the great white shark. Great whites grow to be 40 feet long and have razor-sharp teeth.

Is it true that sharks never stop moving?

Yes, sharks must move in order to breathe. There are two tiny holes on either side of a shark's head, and the shark must get water into these holes to breathe. The shark does this by swimming and moving water around its head. The water goes into the holes, and the shark takes oxygen from it as it passes over the gills. The water then goes out the shark's gill slits.

Do the same fish live in oceans as in lakes and rivers?

No, different types of fish live in the salty ocean water than the kinds that need fresh water. Some types of fish—like some sharks and salmon—can live in either type of water, but most fish can't.

Why do turtles have shells?

Turtles have shells for protection. They are like underwater soldiers wearing plates of armor. When a turtle senses danger, it pulls its head and legs inside its shell until the coast is clear. Then it pokes out its head and its legs, and goes slowly about its business again.

Are lobsters fish?

No, lobsters belong to the family of crustaceans, not to the family of fish. Shrimps and crabs are also crustaceans. They all have hardened shell-like outer skins that they break out of and leave behind from time to time. When their skin underneath finds itself on top, it hardens up and becomes the tough coat we call the shell.

Why does an octopus have so many arms?

The octopus needs its arms for many things. There are round suction cups on the undersides of the arms that grip the slippery rocks underwater so the octopus can walk or glide with ease. The arms feel and taste the things around them. The octopus catches food with its arms, too (mostly crabs, clams and lobsters), and it uses its powerful arms to crack open shells to get to the meat inside. When an octopus fights, it wraps its arms—or tentacles, as they are called—around its enemies and squeezes the life out of them.

Are whales fish?

No, whales look something like fish and live in the sea, but whales belong to the family of mammals. Some other sea mammals are porpoises, seals, and sea cows.

How big are whales?

Different types of whales are different sizes, but the biggest is the blue whale—100 feet long and as heavy as 180 tons. The blue whale is the biggest animal to ever live, bigger even than the hugest dinosaurs that used to roam the earth.

If a whale isn't a fish, how does it breathe under water?

Since whales are mammals and not fish, they do not have gills and do not breathe under water. They have lungs and must come up to the surface of the water for air. They take deep breaths that they can hold for up to two hours.

Is it true that whales talk?

Yes, whales do talk in their own way. They make noises and chatter to each other with squeaks and clicks and moans. But whales also make sounds that they use to help them find things in the water. They make a noise and wait for its echo to return. Whales can judge the distance that the sound traveled before it reached the object that sent back the echo.

ON THE EARTH

How old is the earth?

The earth is about 4 billion, 5 hundred million years old.

Why don't we fall off the earth?

All objects in the universe have an inner force called gravity that pulls other objects toward them, down toward their center. The bigger an object, the greater is its power to pull. The earth's gravity keeps us on the earth by always drawing us toward the center of the earth. But it doesn't pull on us so much that we become uncomfortable—it pulls just the right amount.

What is the earth made of?

The earth is made mostly of rock. There are three basic layers of rock that lead down to the very center of the earth. The *crust* is the outermost layer, made up of the hard kind of rock we find on the earth's surface. The *crust* goes down for 20 or 30 miles, and begins to get very hot after the first 5 miles. The next layer of rock is the *mantle,* which goes down for 1800 miles. The *mantle* has lots of iron and minerals in it. The deeper down you go, the hotter it is. Down toward the center is a final layer called the *core,* which is made up of both melted and very hard rock.

What's a mineral?

Minerals are the stuff that rocks are made of—and so, minerals are the basic material that the earth is made of, too. The different combinations of minerals in rocks are what determines the type of rock it is. Some minerals you might know are gold, silver, and copper.

Are diamonds minerals?

Yes, diamonds are minerals. Diamond is the hardest type of rock there is, and it is the most valuable, too. Because the diamond's crystal structure is so beautiful, people want to wear diamonds for jewelry, and because it is so hard, diamond is useful for industrial reasons.

Where did mountains come from?

Mountains are the result of many millions of years of the earth's crust crinkling and wrinkling up. The rocks beneath the earth's surface are under a great deal of pressure because of all the weight pushing down on them, and sometimes they must shift their positions the way people do to get more comfortable after sitting in the same place too long. When this happens, everything shifts—including the earth's crust, which tries to "fit" around the inside earth as best it can. It cracks and slowly, over the years, gets pushed up in large chunks—as big as mountains.

What's a volcano?

A volcano is like a mountain with an opening at the top. This hole is called a crater, and it leads all the way down inside the earth to where there is the layer of melted rock, steam and hot gases. The pressure is so great there that sometimes it forces lava (the melted rock) to rise and pour out of the top. Gases and steam and hard pieces of broken-off rock come out, too. You can climb some volcanoes and peek over the top, but don't lean too far. . .

What's an earthquake?

When the pressure on the rocks in the earth becomes very great, they sometimes crack. The earth shakes when this happens. When the cracks are big enough to affect the top layer (the crust) and the earth's surface splits apart, this is an earthquake. Once the crust has a crack—or fault—in it, earthquakes will be more likely to happen there in the future. During an earthquake, big chunks of the ground can break apart and move into new positions. Sometimes buildings will fall over—even mountains may come down. But usually the ground just shakes a little bit.

What's a jungle?

A jungle is a place where it is very hot and moist all the year round. The trees, plants, and bushes grow so thick that you have to carve a path to get through.

Why is it hot in the jungle?

Most of the jungles in the world lie near the equator, which is the place on earth that is always nearest to the sun. The temperature is usually 80 degrees Fahrenheit, but often it gets much, much hotter than that.

What animals live in the jungle?

Many different types of animals live in the jungle—apes and monkeys, pigs, alligators, rhinoceri, hippopotami, snakes and leopards—just about any animal that can survive in a thick-growing, moist environment. Most of the animals, like the apes and monkeys, live in the trees, but rhinoceri, hippos and alligators soak in the rivers and marshes, trying to keep cool. Snakes slither around everywhere. There are many beautifully colored birds in the trees—lots of parrots and, in some jungles, zippy little hummingbirds darting to and fro. Insects live in the jungle, too; there are always ants and spiders and termites and mosquitos crawling and flying about.

Is it true that some tree animals NEVER come down to the ground during their lives?

Yes, it is true. Many monkeys spend their whole lives in the green treetops, swinging through the branches. Everything they need grows or lives there, so there is no need for them to fight their way through the thick leaves down to the earth.

What grows in the jungle?

Many different kinds of plants and trees grow in the jungle. There are lots of pretty orchids, one of which has the vanilla flavor in it that we use to make vanilla ice cream and other vanilla-flavored treats. In one jungle in Sumatra the largest of all flowers, the rafflesia, grows as big as 13 feet across its center, and weighs as much as 15 pounds. Lots of trees that bear delicious fruits like mangoes and bananas grow in the jungle. Cacao trees grow in jungles, too—that's where we get cacao beans that we use to make cocoa and chocolate.

Do people live in the jungle?

There are some scattered tribes of jungle people who survive by eating plants and hunting animals. Monkeys, pigs, birds and other small animals often end up as their dinners. Sometimes insects will do for a meal, too.

What is a desert?

A desert is a very dry place where it hardly ever rains. Ordinarily, air contains moisture, but desert air is different. Many deserts have big mountain ranges between them and the ocean. The air from ocean breezes must travel over these mountains to get to the desert on the other side. As the air climbs up the mountains, it gets colder and colder, and the moisture in it turns to snow— and it falls. Sometimes the moisture never even makes it to the mountaintop. It usually doesn't make it to the other side at all.

How hot does the desert get?

In El Azizia, Libya, the desert gets as hot as 136 degrees Fahrenheit. California's Death Valley gets almost that hot in the summer, too.

Do plants grow in the desert?

Yes. Special types of plants have learned to live in the desert on very little water. Cactus plants, for example, have fat stems in which they store water. Even during a long, dry spell, a cactus will not dry up. Some other desert plants, such as the yucca plant, have roots that they send way down into the earth to search for water. Others only live for a short period of time during the "rainy" season in the desert, when there is water for them to flourish.

Do animals live in the desert?

Many animals live in the desert, but they are hard to find if you go out to look for them. Some are sand-colored for protection. Others come out only at night because it is so hot during the day. Some desert creatures have a reverse hibernation pattern from most animals—they sleep during the hottest parts of the year and wake up when the desert is cooler. Coyotes and foxes roam the deserts seeking waterholes. Toads and frogs are desert dwellers, and so are the lizards and snakes you will see dart out now and then. Ants and spiders and wasps live in deserts, too.

Is the desert hot at night, too?

Not usually. Deserts need the heat of the sun to stay hot, so when night falls, the desert gets cold. In other hot places the air stays warm at night because the moisture in it helps to hold the heat from the day. But desert air is so dry that it can't hold the sun's warmth from the afternoon. The temperature may drop from over a hundred degrees Fahrenheit in the day to —53 degrees Fahrenheit at night. In more humid deserts, the drop in temperature is less dramatic during the summer months.

What was the Great Ice Age?

About a million years ago, the earth began to get colder and colder, until ice covered all of the land in the entire northern part of the world: all of Canada, the northern United States, all of Scandinavia, Denmark, the Netherlands and northern Europe, Russia and Poland. No one knows exactly why this happened. Even though the weather warmed up and melted some of the ice four times during this period of time, the cold always came back and froze everything over again. These million years—up to the present day—are called the Great Ice Age.

What's a glacier? How does one move?

A glacier is a mass of moving ice. It is at least 1000 feet thick, and often a few miles thick. It may be big enough to cover an entire continent of land. Glaciers form when snow builds up in the valleys between high mountains. It is so cold that the snow doesn't have the chance to melt, and it keeps getting packed down until it turns to ice. When the weight of the ice mass is great enough, the pull of gravity and the pressure from the top of the glacier begin to affect the ice at the bottom. It gets "squeezed out" and begins to move downhill.

IN THE SKY

What is a star?

A star is a huge ball made up of very hot gases that give off light. The sun is a star. All the twinkling points of light in the night sky are stars, too, but since they are so far away from the earth, their light doesn't seem as bright as the sun's.

How many stars are there?

No one knows for sure, because every time scientists invent stronger telescopes, they discover more stars. But if you look up into the sky yourself on a clear night, you can probably see about 2,000 stars.

What's the nearest star?

The sun is the nearest star to the earth. It is almost 93 million miles away and yet still shines brightly enough to make the earth so hot in the summer that you need a dip in the cool sea to stay comfortable.

What's the Milky Way?

The Milky Way is the name of the family of stars that our sun belongs to. All the stars your eye can see are part of the Milky Way, and there are many more in it that are too far away for your eye to find. If you could travel out into space beyond the Milky Way and look back at it, it would look like a star-studded belt with a big round glittery buckle.

Why do stars twinkle?

Stars are very far away from the earth, and their light must travel through a lot of space before you can see it. As the light comes down to earth, it passes through the atmosphere, which is the thicker, moister air that surrounds our planet. This makes the light quiver, or twinkle.

What is a falling star?

A falling star isn't really a star at all—it is a meteor. Meteors are small masses of rock and particles from outer space that get very hot and burn fiercely when they suddenly hit the thicker air surrounding the earth and enter the earth's atmosphere. As meteors fall to the earth, we see their fiery light shoot across the sky, and this is what we call a falling star. But as they fall, they burn out—usually before they reach the ground. If you make a wish when you see a falling star, it is supposed to bring good luck. Try it!

Why does the moon shine?

The moon shines because it reflects light from the sun. The moon does not give off any light of its own.

Who was the first person on the moon?

On July 20, 1969, Astronaut Neil Armstrong took the first walk on the moon. Astronaut Edwin Aldrin joined him later, while Michael Collins orbited the moon in Apollo 11's command module.

How long did it take to fly to the moon?

Armstrong, Aldrin, and Collins spent 4 days aboard the Apollo 11 spacecraft flying to the moon.

What is a comet?

A comet is made up of dust and frozen gases and is often compared to a dirty snowball in space. Comets travel around the sun, as the planets do, but comets orbit in paths that are shaped like hotdogs instead of circles. As a comet moves close to the sun, some of its frozen gases and ice become vapor, or steam, and when sunlight passes through the vapor, it looks like it glows. The force of the sun's rays actually pushes these gases away, giving the comet a tail that glows, too.

What are planets?

Planets are the roundish-shaped balls that circle the sun.
Together with the sun, the nine planets make up what we call
the solar system. Scientists believe that long ago the sun was
born in space when some gas and dust particles came together
and began to spin. They kept getting hotter and hotter and
spinning faster and faster until they were a hot swirling cloud.
Parts of the edge of the cloud broke away and began to swing
around the outside. These became the planets.

Where are the planets?

The planets are in space, in orbit around the sun. Mercury is
closest to the sun—only 36 million miles away, so it is very hot
all year round. Venus is next to Mercury, and it shows up as the
brightest object in our night sky, even though it is surrounded by
lemon-yellow clouds that cover its surface from our sight. Earth
is next in the solar system, the only planet with the right
conditions for life. That's where we live—on the third planet
from the sun. Then comes Mars, a planet that often looks like a
reddish ball in the sky. Scientists have recently discovered that
there are huge volcanoes and enormous canyons on Mars,
although no one is sure yet how they were formed. Jupiter is the
next orbiting planet, with a mysterious red-colored spot and
several colored bands that wrap around it. Saturn, famous for its
colored rings, comes after Jupiter. Then Uranus, Neptune, and
Pluto—all very far away, and very cold because they get little
heat from the sun.

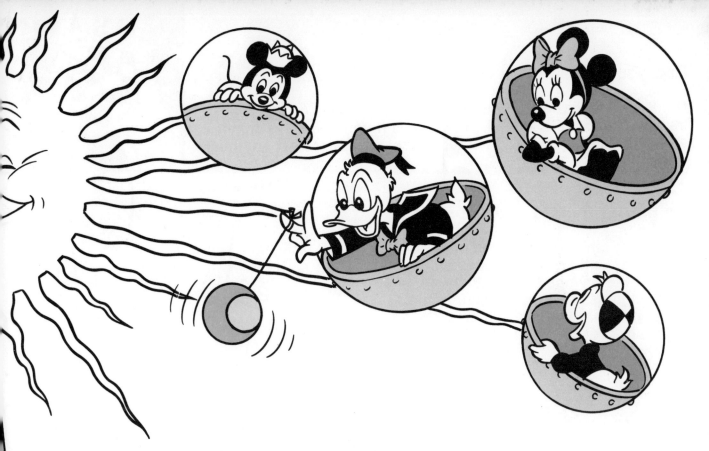

Why don't the planets collide?

Each planet sticks to its own path of travel around the
sun. These paths, or orbits, are millions of miles apart, so they
never cross or even come close to each other. Because the sun's
gravitational field—the area affected by the sun's force of
gravity—is steady, it keeps the planets revolving in a constant,
orderly pattern.

What does Earth look like in outer space?

Earth can only be seen in outer space when the sun reflects
light on it. If you were on Venus, the earth would be the
brightest object in the sky. But to really see the earth's surface,
you would need a telescope and some luck to find a clear spot
in the clouds that surround our planet. Then you might see
white caps on Earth—the snow and ice at the North or South Pole.

How's the weather in outer space?

Weather is a word that tells what the air is like—if it has a lot of
moisture in it, or if it is very cold, or if there are gusty winds or
no winds at all. Since there is no air in outer space, there is no
weather, either. Outer space stays very cold, except around
the stars, which are so hot they warm up the area close to them.

Can you hear in outer space?

No. Sound is carried to your ears by air vibrations (which are invisible, but would look like wavy lines if you could see them), and since there is no air in outer space, you can't hear anything.

Do planes fly into outer space?

No. There isn't enough air in outer space for planes, either! Planes need air around their wings to keep them up, and their engines need the oxygen from air to keep running. Above 20 miles, the air gets too thin. Planes must fly below this 20-mile limit.

Then how does a rocket get into outer space?

Rockets carry the fuel they need for their engines with them—they don't rely on the air outside. To get beyond the gravitational pull of Earth, a rocket must travel at a speed of at least 25,000 miles per hour. It takes a very big push for this to happen! There is a special way that rockets create this power. They burn their fuel inside to form hot gases. Then they wait until the gases are ready to burst out, and they open a little hole in the back end of the rocket. Whoosh! The rocket gets pushed forward and zooms off into space.

Does anybody live in outer space?

It is possible that there may be other forms of life somewhere in the universe, but so far we haven't seen or heard from them. There are many billions of stars in the universe too far away from Earth for us to tell with the equipment we now have. No one knows for sure if there is life on the planets that circle other stars the way we circle the sun. We are fairly certain now that earth is the only planet in our solar system that has life on it. But keep your ears, eyes and mind open, and perhaps you will find out otherwise.

Both the United States and the Soviet Union are planning to build huge space homes called colonies where people can live and work in outer space. The colonies will have everything that people living there will need to function in a world of their own far away from Mother Earth. The people won't take canned food with them, but they will take all the necessary materials to grow their own food and raise their own animals. The colonies will orbit the earth and use the sun as their source of energy.

Huge, ringlike structures called space stations may also provide homes in outer space. Space stations will orbit the earth close by—only a few hundred miles away. Scientists can work on special research projects there, and travelers will be able to stop to rest or pick up new equipment for their space cars, or ships, or whatever they are driving.

Do birds fly in space?

No. Birds also need air to move them along and, most importantly, they need air to breathe!

How high do birds fly?

Most birds fly about 5,000 feet up in the air, but some storks and cranes have been seen flying over the Himalaya Mountains, which means they were flying above 20,000 feet!

What makes a bird a bird?

Robins fly, insects fly, butterflies fly—are they all birds because they fly? No—only animals with feathers are birds. It doesn't matter if it can fly or sing, if it has feathers, it's a bird. All birds have two wings, two legs and a beak where their mouths are.

Do all birds fly?

No. Chickens don't fly—their wings aren't large enough to lift their bodies off the ground. They flap around a bit, though. An ostrich can't fly, either—it runs where it goes, and it can run faster than some horses. Penquins don't fly; they are water birds, and their wings are flattened down like paddles.

How fast do birds fly?

Certain types of swifts have been seen flying past an airplane— at the rate of almost 200 miles per hour. When a hummingbird hovers, or stays above the same spot without moving forward or back, it flies the slowest of any bird—0 miles per hour! There is no average speed. Birds can fly at different speeds at different times.

Are there any birds that can fly backward?

Yes. After hummingbirds hover over flowers and get the nectar out of them, they fly backward away from the flower.

Why do birds have beaks?

Birds have beaks to make up for not having hands. Different birds have different types of beaks, depending on what they eat. Woodpeckers have sharp, pointed beaks so they can find insects inside trees. Ducks have flattened bills that let them scoop up small animals and plants in shallow water.

When do baby birds learn to fly?

Baby birds learn to fly when their wings have grown large enough and strong enough to try out. The babies start to get restless in the nest and begin to test their wings by stretching them out and flapping them in place. The mother and father birds will usually watch their babies getting ready, and they will fly around nearby to show the little ones that it's not so hard. Soon one little bird will jump up in the air and start flapping—then they will all be flying about like young pros. If there is one brother or sister a little unsure about the first jump, it will get an encouraging push out of the nest, anyway!

How do birds find their way?

Scientists have several ideas about this, but nothing has been proven yet. One theory is that birds see very well, and they spot landmarks as they fly. But they must have very good memories to remember where they've been and what their landmarks were! Whatever the reason, birds very rarely get lost and have an excellent sense of direction.

STRANGE AND CURIOUS BEASTS

What were dinosaurs?

Dinosaurs were ancient reptiles that lived about 165 million years ago. Reptiles are scaly-covered, cold-blooded creatures that crawl or swim, like lizards and snakes. Some dinosaurs were only one or two feet long and fairly harmless, but many were very big and fierce. The largest dinosaur that ever lived was called Diplodocus and grew to be 80 feet long.

What does the word "dinosaur" mean?

The word *dinosaur* comes from the Greek language, and it means "terrible lizard." Some dinosaurs certainly deserved this name. Tyrannosaurus Rex, or "King of the Giant Reptiles," was about 30 feet long and had big, sharp teeth that were eight inches long. When Tyrannosaurus Rex stood up on his hind legs, he was as tall as a two-story house.

What did dinosaurs eat?

Dinosaurs liked different types of food, depending on the kind of dinosaur they were. Some, like Tyrannosaurus Rex, were meat-eaters and preyed on smaller dinosaurs. Others, like Trachodon, ate swamp plants. Mosasaurs, which were sea lizards, thought fish made the best meal.

What did dinosaurs look like?

Stegosaurus was a dinosaur covered with spikes and horny plates. Some dinosaurs lived in the sea, so they had legs like paddles. Triceratops had three horns on its head. Brontosaurus, whose name means "thundering lizard," was a swamp dweller whose body was as long as a whale's and weighed almost 20 tons. It had a long snaky neck with a tiny little head. One dinosaur—Brachiosaurus—was so heavy (35 to 85 tons) that it couldn't stand up on its own two feet. It had to spend all of its time in the water to keep from falling over!

How do we know what dinosaurs looked like?

When dinosaurs died, their bodies sank into the mud and earth and made impressions, or pressed-down pictures, of the way they looked. As time passed, the dinosaurs' teeth and skin and some of their bones turned to stone. Millions of years later man began to dig up traces of this ancient world buried in stone. In many places around the world enough bones have been found at the same sites to allow scientists to rebuild the skeletons of lots of dinosaurs. You can see them today in museums.

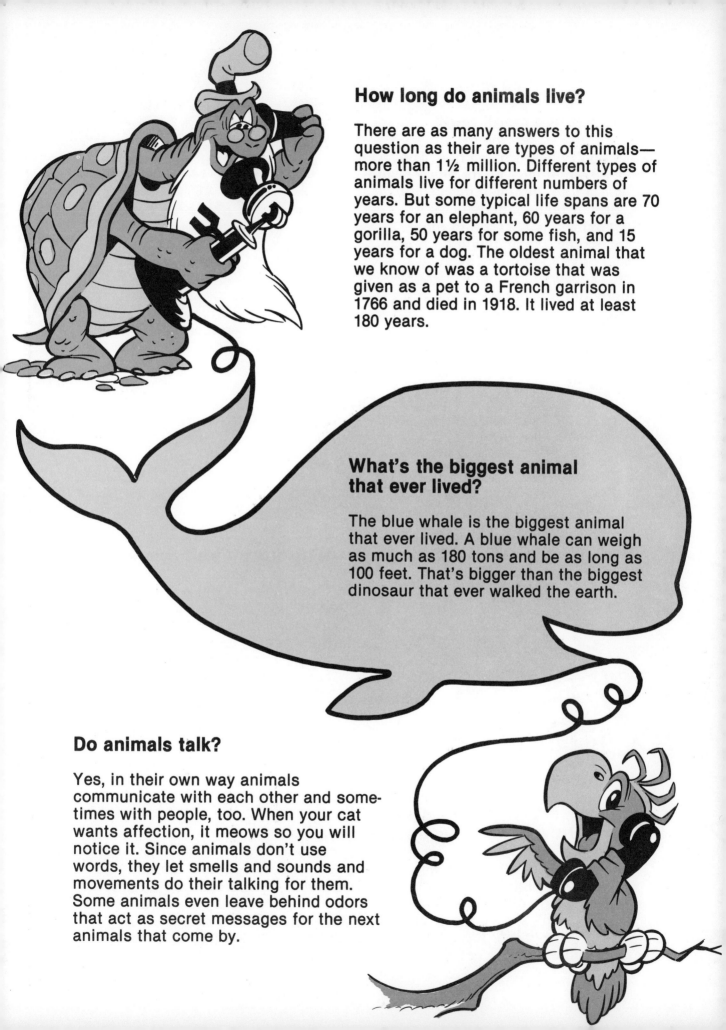

How long do animals live?

There are as many answers to this question as their are types of animals—more than 1½ million. Different types of animals live for different numbers of years. But some typical life spans are 70 years for an elephant, 60 years for a gorilla, 50 years for some fish, and 15 years for a dog. The oldest animal that we know of was a tortoise that was given as a pet to a French garrison in 1766 and died in 1918. It lived at least 180 years.

What's the biggest animal that ever lived?

The blue whale is the biggest animal that ever lived. A blue whale can weigh as much as 180 tons and be as long as 100 feet. That's bigger than the biggest dinosaur that ever walked the earth.

Do animals talk?

Yes, in their own way animals communicate with each other and sometimes with people, too. When your cat wants affection, it meows so you will notice it. Since animals don't use words, they let smells and sounds and movements do their talking for them. Some animals even leave behind odors that act as secret messages for the next animals that come by.

Why do skunks smell bad?

Skunks don't always smell bad. They only smell when they are in danger, and they give off an unpleasant odor for protection. It tastes as awful as it smells, and if it is sprayed in the skunk's enemy's face, it will burn painfully and drive the enemy away. It is a very effective way for them to keep strangers and uninvited guests at a distance.

Why do camels have humps?

Camels live in deserts where food and water is often hard to find, so they have to be good at storing extra food inside their bodies to get them through the tough times. They store food in their humps in the form of fat, and they use it up as they need it. Some camels have only one hump instead of two, and they are called dromedaries. They live mostly in Africa and North India.

How big are elephants?

Elephants are the biggest land animals. They stand about 11 feet high and weigh three to four tons. Baby elephants already weigh close to 200 pounds at birth. Elephants are so big they aren't afraid of any other animals—except for snakes, which love to bite the tip of the elephant's trunk as it pokes around in the grass.

What do elephants eat?

Elephants eat leaf buds and leaves off of trees. They love berries and grass and grass-sprouts. When food is difficult to find, they will dig up roots and chew on them for the juice.

What are an elephant's tusks for?

Elephants use their tusks like teeth and hands. They use tusks to pry wood out of trees or the earth, and they also use their tusks to grind food. Tusks are made of ivory and can be as big as 12 feet long. The record weight is 200 pounds. That's a lot of tusk!

What is an elephant's trunk for?

An elephant's trunk is useful for many things. The elephant breathes through it and smells with it, testing the air constantly for new scents. It is like hands for the elephant. It picks leaves and berries off trees. Elephants use their trunks like big drinking straws, too; they take water up into their trunks, then spray it into their mouths. And elephant mothers stroke their babies with their trunks to show they love them.

What is a rhinoceros' horn for?

A rhinoceros uses its horn to get leaves off trees to munch on.
A rhinoceros' horn is to the rhinoceros what an elephant's
tusk is to an elephant. But the rhino's horn is really a hump of
tightly packed hair; it's not made of ivory, like the elephant's tusk,
or of horn, like a deer's antlers.

Why do animals sleep all winter?

Animals sleep all winter, or hibernate, to help them get through the
winter when it is very cold and food is hard to find. Some
animals eat so much in the fall, getting ready to hibernate,
they are too fat to move all winter, anyway!

Do they fall asleep right away?

No, they take some time settling into the new homes they have
chosen for their winter's sleep. They stay closer and closer to
home and take more and more naps until they finally fall into
one long, deep winter's sleep.

How soundly do they sleep?

It depends on the animal. Reptiles and insects, for example, sleep so soundly that they can't wake up, even if they need to, in the middle of the winter. Bears sleep on and off, and are easily awakened—especially mother bears. A mother grizzly will wake up if something or someone comes into the den where she and her cubs are snoozing. But she can go right back into a deep sleep when the danger is gone. Chipmunks store up grains and nuts in their grass-covered burrows, and they wake up to snack when they get hungry.

How do hibernating animals know when to wake up?

Some animals wake up only when the temperature outside becomes warm enough to "thaw" them out. Fish sleeping in the mud on the bottom of a pond get a sudden fresh supply of oxygen when the pond melts, and this gives their bodies the energy to wake up. Once asleep, deep hibernators, such as woodchucks, hedgehogs and squirrels, will not wake up for a good six months, but after that their own bodies know it is time to get up. They have a special layer of body fat that turns itself into energy at this point and it warms them up enough to get them out and moving around in the world again.

What do bears eat?

Different types of bears eat different things. Panda bears, which
live in bamboo forests in the high mountains of western China,
eat only bamboo. Giant brown bears of Alaska come down to the
sea in the summertime to catch salmon with their paws and
feast on it until fall. Grizzlies like acorns and berries and ants,
and sometimes small animals. Polar bears love seal and walrus
meat. They sneak up on unsuspecting seals and walruses
napping on the ice and. . .POUNCE!

Can bears swim and climb trees?

Polar bears are the best swimmers. Most bears only climb trees
when they are young, but the black bears of North America are
tree-climbers all of their lives.

How do polar bears stay warm in the cold
northern winters?

They have very heavy coats of fur that keep them warm. Since
their coats are the same color as the snow, other animals can't
see them very well. So their coats protect them from cold and
danger, too!

What keeps polar bears from slipping on the ice?

Their feet are covered with stiff fur that lets them "grip" instead of slip!

Do bears make marks on trees?

Yes, all bears except polar bears leave their marks on trees. They stand by a tree and stretch up with their front paws as high as they can go. Then they scratch and bite the bark, leaving their autograph of tooth and claw. Sometimes another bear will come by later and try to leave a mark higher up on the tree, to show that he was better. Marked trees are called "bear trees."

Why do beavers build dams?

Beavers build dams to make the water where they want to live deep enough for their homes. If the water is deep, their homes will be good protection for them. Then, when they go to get food and wood on land and see danger coming, they can swim to their "castle" and leave their enemies on the other side of the "moat." Also, if a pond is deep enough, it will only freeze on top. Then, if a beaver must go to shore, it can go out the underwater door and swim beneath the ice—out of the reach of hungry animals slinking across the ice hunting for food. But beavers try to stock their mud-homes with enough bark and branches to last them all winter long.

Why does a cat purr?

Cats purr to show they are happy and feel content. No one is really sure how the cat makes the noise, but some scientists think cats have an extra set of vocal chords in their throats that they move in a certain way—or vibrate —to make the "purr."

Do cats have nine lives?

No, cats only live once. The reason people say that cats have nine lives is because they will almost always land on their feet when dropped from a height, and many times, when they might have died, they really get another chance to "live" again. The real reason cats flop over to land on their feet is because their spines—though flexible—are not very strong and the cat knows it must protect its back by NOT landing on it.

Why do dogs have fleas?

Fleas are insects that live on animals and birds. They feed off their blood. A flea is very small, like a grain of wild rice—1/10 of an inch long. A flea bites the animal that it lives on, then crawls and jumps around in the animal's fur until it is hungry again. Then it dives in for another bite. These bites itch. That is why you often see dogs scratching furiously when they have fleas.

Why does a kangaroo have a pouch?

Kangaroos belong to a group of animals called marsupials. All marsupials have pouches. When marsupial babies are born, they aren't developed enough to live without first getting some extra special care from their mothers. Inside the mother's pouch are nipples for the babies to suck on for milk, and soon the babies grow into little animals. They are born only an inch long, but within six months they gain almost 10 pounds and are large enough to hop out of the pouch and come back only when they are scared or want to go for a fun ride!

Why do opossums hang upside down?

Opossums—the only marsupials that live in the United States—hang upside down for two reasons. One is to reach their favorite fruit, the persimmon. The opossum grasps a branch with its tail and one back foot and hangs head-down. Using a front foot like a hand, the opossum reaches out and—pluck!—grabs its prize.

The other reason opossums hang upside down is for protection. "Playing possum" is what we call it when someone goes limp and pretends to be dead—because this is what an opossum will do when it senses danger. When the enemy has passed, the opossum comes back to life and quickly scrambles away.

What's the difference between a crocodile and an alligator?

Crocodiles are smaller and quicker than alligators, and they move more easily. Crocodiles are usually thinner, too, and their snouts come to a point in front. Alligator snouts are blunt, or squared off at the front end. Alligators are usually blackish-colored, and crocodiles are olive or gray. Although crocodiles have fewer teeth than alligators, these teeth are sharper and longer and are seen outside the crocodile's mouth. Crocodiles live in salt-water swamps; alligators prefer fresh water.

How big are frogs?

They range in size from the giant Goliath frog, which can be 12 inches long and weigh as much as 7 pounds, to the littlest one-inch tree frogs.

What's the difference between a frog and a toad?

Although both frogs and toads are amphibians—which means that they can live in water or on land—there are differences between them. Many of the differences are on the inside, not the outside, but there are some you can see. Frogs are skinnier and have smoother skin. Toads look fat and warty. Some frogs that live in warm climates have even learned to climb, so they can spend their time up in the trees, jumping around on the ground, or splashing in the water.

Can you get warts from touching frogs or toads?

No, touching frogs or toads will not give you warts. There is a poisonous fluid in the bumps on a toad's skin that comes out when the toad is frightened, but it will not harm you—only the toad's enemies. Usually people are polite enough to toads to avoid being sprayed, anyway. But if you do touch the toad's bumps, you should wash your hands right away, since the poisonous liquid could sting if it got in your eyes.

Why do chameleons change color?

Chameleons change color according to their moods—if they are frightened and want to hide from their enemies, they become the same color as whatever they are standing on—brown for tree trunks, green for leaves. Then no one can find them!

Are all snakes dangerous?

No. There are about 2,400 different types of snakes, and only 200 of them are poisonous. Most snakes bite people only when they are scared and feel threatened by them.

How do snakes eat?

Snakes have very interesting mouths. Their jaws open up so wide they can swallow their food whole, even if it is bigger than the snake's whole head. A typical snake dinner is a couple of small animals like rats and mice, insects, birds, or frogs. Some snakes have fangs, which are poisonous teeth, and when they bite down, their victims die right away. Then the snake gobbles them whole. The snake's body will stretch when it must to fit in the meal, and it must take weeks or months to fully digest. Pythons and constrictor snakes wrap their bodies around their prey and suffocate them to death—then they eat them.

Why do bugs have antennae?

Bugs have antennae for the same reasons that we have our eyes and ears and noses and mouths and hands—to tell us about the world around us. Most antennae have tiny, sensitive hairs on them that know how to "smell" and "taste." These hairs also "hear" by picking up sounds. Insects use their antennae to feel around them, and to test out new territory. Sometimes, when you see the antennae waving in the air, the bug is trying to find out about YOU!

How do flies walk upside down?

Flies have feet that are padded on the bottom. When the fly walks, the pads let out a sticky fluid that keeps its feet attached to the surface it is on—even if it is the ceiling and the fly is upside down.

Why do crickets make so much noise?

It's male crickets you hear making all that racket, trying to impress female friends. Since their chirping sound is what lady crickets like best, the male crickets rub their wings together to make it. It's really a love song that isn't sung at all. But it works!

What makes a firefly light up?

No one knows for sure why fireflies light up, but it is probably their way of showing off to attract mates. Fireflies have two different kinds of liquid in their bodies, and when they both mix with air, the firefly brightens up and flashes in the dark.

Why do spiders spin webs?

Spiders spin webs to trap food—beetles and flies and mosquitoes and any other bug that will wander into the web.

What is the web made of?

The web is woven out of silk thread.

Where does the silk come from?

The spider itself makes the silk. Silk starts out as a fluid inside the spider's body. There are tiny openings at the top of the spider's body, called spinnerets, where the silk comes out. When it reaches the air, it hardens into a thread.

How does a spider spin a web?

The spider weaves the silk thread back and forth to build a web. If the spider is building a web on rock, it will press its spinnerets to the rock and then run off, and the silk will reel out behind it. If the spider darts back and forth, the silk threads will stick together and make a trap for unsuspecting ants and bugs to crawl into. Some spiders, called orb spiders, stretch their silk lines between trees and weave big round webs.

What happens to a spider's web in the rain?

Most webs are strong enough to stay put during a storm. Others will wash away, and the spider will have to build a new web.

Can a spider fix a broken web?

Yes. The spider mends the web by running back and forth over the damaged area and laying down new threads to stick to the broken ones. This is their way of "sewing" the web back together.

How do bees make honey?

Honeybees are the only kind of bee that makes honey. A honeybee's tongue becomes long enough to reach deep down inside flowers to suck up the sweet liquid that flowers make, called nectar. The honeybee has a special stomach to keep the nectar in, once it has been swallowed, and there the nectar turns into a liquid-sweet honey. When the bee has drunk its fill of nectar, it flies back to its hive, sucks the honey up out of its stomach, and stores it in the little compartments you see in a honeycomb. The liquidy honey becomes a little thicker there as it dries out, and then it is delicious and very good to eat.

Why do bees sting?

Bees sting when they are mad, or scared, or hurt. Their stinger is their only weapon for protection.

Do all bees sting?

No. Some bees don't sting at all, but most do. Honeybees only sting once, since their stingers have hooks that sink into the bodies of whatever they sting, and then the stinger gets stuck there. When the honeybee flies away, its stinger gets pulled out of its body. A bumblebee's stinger, however, has no hooks and can be used again and again.

WHAT ARE YOU MADE OF?

What is a skeleton?

A skeleton is the framework of your body—all 206 of your bones joined together in one piece.

What are muscles for?

Muscles help give shape to your body, and they help you move. Some muscles follow your orders—such as when you want to lift your arm or run. Others, like your heart, work on their own without your having to give them any instructions at all.

How many muscles do we have?

There are more than 500 different muscles in the human body. The smallest muscles you have makes the edges of your mouth curve up into a smile. The largest lets you jump high in the air.

Why do we need skin?

Skin is the ideal substance to cover the human body. It is tough enough to protect the person inside from harmful germs and from getting hurt. It's flexible enough to let us move around, and if it gets cut, it can heal itself. Skin also lets us know what things "feel like" when we touch them—how hot or cold they are, if they are pressing on us, if they hurt. And skin is such a perfect covering for us that it always keeps the same amount of moisture and warmth inside the body, regardless of the weather outside.

Why do people have different color skin?

There is something in skin called *pigment* that determines what color it will be. Pigment comes in two colors, brown and yellow. People who have a lot of brown pigment in their skin and very little yellow will have black skin. White skin comes from a combination of the two. Oriental people have much more yellow than brown pigment in their skin. The amount of pigment is inherited, or passed down, from your parents.

What are freckles?

Freckles are little orange-brown spots that many people have on their faces, shoulders, and other parts of their bodies. They come from a certain substance called *melanin,* a skin pigment, which gets especially active when the sun's rays give it extra energy to work. Freckles run in families, so if your parents and sisters and brothers have freckles, you probably will, too.

What are fingernails?

Nails on your fingers and on your toes are really special hardened layers of skin, designed to protect the soft parts of your hands and feet beneath them. Each nail has a root that lies deep in the skin and is attached to the bone in each finger and toe.

Why do we have hair?

We have hair for protection and warmth. Originally, when man lived outdoors most of the time, hair was necessary for survival against the cold and wind and rain. It is still important nowadays, but not quite so much.

Why doesn't it hurt when hair gets cut?

Hair is actually a collection of dead cells that have been pushed out of their home base, the root. Since hair is a long line of dead cells, it has no feelings and doesn't hurt when cut.

Why are some people blond and others brunette?

Hair color is inherited—it depends on the color of hair your parents have. In the same way that there is pigment in skin, there is pigment in hair roots that determines the color. Some people have yellow and others brown, and some have a combination of the two. When people get old, and the pigment gets tired and stops being made, hair has no color and is white. Curly and straight hair are also inherited. Most people in the world have curly hair.

What are teeth made of?

Teeth are made of a special type of very hard bone, and covered by a protective substance called enamel.

Why do we get cavities?

When food particles get stuck in between teeth, they bring bacteria, or bad germs, in with them. The bacteria attack the enamel of the teeth, and when they break through and reach the soft part inside your tooth, a cavity results. That's why it is important to brush your teeth often, and especially after eating—to make sure no food wedges its way in between your teeth to stay there overnight—or for good.

Why do we get toothaches?

Toothaches are a signal to let you know that there is a very deep cavity in your tooth. At the very bottom of each tooth is a very sensitive spot—and when the cavity reaches it, it hurts!

Why does your heart beat?

Your heart beats because it is a pump—one that keeps blood flowing to all parts of your body at all times. The beat you hear is the sound of the different parts of the heart doing their work. There are four parts, called chambers, and there are doors, called valves, which open and close between them. As the chambers tighten up and then relax, they push the blood in and out of the heart in spurts. You hear this, plus the opening and closing of the valves, when you hear the "lub-dub" sound.

Why do we need blood?

Blood is the human body's river of life—it carries all of the precious substances that the body's cells need for nourishment and well-being. When you breathe in air, the *red blood cells* take out the oxygen and deliver it to all the parts of your body. When the food you eat has been broken down into chemicals in your stomach, your bloodstream carries it to hungry cells. There are some things that your cells don't need, called waste materials, and your bloodstream will take them away and get rid of them for you. Also in the blood are *white blood cells* that fight infection, and tiny little cells called *platelets* that make your blood clot, or stop flowing, when you cut yourself.

Why does your face get red when you are embarrassed?

Emotions very often show up on your face—in the way you look and also in the color of your skin. When you get embarrassed, the little muscles that surround the blood vessels in your face and neck open up to let more blood in and your face shows it. It gets all red and hot. You can't hide it, even though you might like to. It happens to us all!

Why do you pant when you run?

When you need more energy than usual, your body works harder to give it to you. It needs extra oxygen to help release the energy stored in your cells. If you breathe fast and take in more air, you bring in more oxygen, too. Then you can make extra energy for yourself. But your body knows this on its own without you reminding it, so it makes sure in its own way that you breathe hard when you run.

Why do you see your breath on a cold day?

Your breath comes from inside your body where it is warm and moist. When you open your mouth and this warm, moist air hits the cold frosty air outside, it suddenly cools down. In the cooling process the moisture becomes vapor (like steam) and it looks like you are making a little cloud. It disappears quickly, but you make another one right away with your next breath.

Why do you blink?

Blinking is a reflex, or an automatic action, that your eyes make to keep themselves moist and protected from harmful material, like dust or sand. When you blink, you actually draw the eye's special watery solution—tears—over the eye, to wash it out.

Why do you cry?

Usually you cry when you are feeling sad, or hurt, or whenever your feelings get so strong inside they fill you up to the top and spill over in tears. Sometimes you cry when you sneeze or cough, too. Your eyes are connected in the back to tubes that also connect to the breathing passages of your nose and throat. So any time you sneeze or cough, you affect the part of your eye that produces tears, and it reacts by making you cry.

What are tears?

When a sensitive part of your eye called the nerve is excited or stirred up by emotions or a sneeze or a cough, or by something that has irritated the eyeball, it responds by telling your eye to produce extra tear fluid so there will be enough to take care of the problem. You always have a certain amount of this tear fluid covering your eye, but you have much more of it when you cry or your eyes tear.

What is pain?

Pain is the way your body tells you that something is wrong and it wants you to make everything OK again. Even though you'd rather not feel pain, it's the way your body talks to you and asks for help. "Nerves" are the parts of your body that "understand" signals like pain or pleasure. They tell your brain where in your body you hurt or feel good. For example, when someone pinches your cheek, your nerves signal your brain that your skin is being squeezed too tight! Your brain will tell you to say "Ouch!" and maybe the pincher will stop pinching. Or, if your belly aches, you can call a doctor to find out what's wrong so you can do whatever you should to make it better again.

WATCH OUT FOR THE ~

Why do we sleep?

Scientists are still not exactly sure why the body needs sleep, but most think sleep is the time your body takes to rest and prepare itself for the next day. If anything needs fixing—if you have a fever or an infection—your body uses the time you are asleep to work on making you healthy again. Although your brain shuts down some of its activities while you sleep, like smelling a neighbor's cooking, or hearing cars outside, there are many things in your body which never stop working, even during sleep. Your heart and breathing continue steadily, and your mind stays busy making dreams.

Do animals sleep?

Yes, almost every kind of animal sleeps. Elephants often sleep standing up, their trunks resting in the fork of a tree. Some animals are "good sleepers" and other ones aren't. Animals that can sleep in protected places (out of the danger of their enemies) can really relax. Cats and dogs and monkeys are good sleepers. Poor sleepers—like rabbits, goats, sheep and fish—must stay alert even when they sleep, because they cannot find adequately safe beds. They must always be able to sense and respond to danger, even when they are resting.

What are dreams?

Dreams are the stories you see, hear, and feel in your mind while you are asleep. Very often the things you did and thought about during the day will appear in your dreams at night. Sometimes you will dream about things you want—and in your dream your wish comes true! That makes you feel good. When you are afraid of something, it will often sneak up in your dreams. You will have a bad dream, or a nightmare. If a dream upsets you too much, you will usually wake yourself up. Then you realize it was only a dream, and the bad feeling will go away soon.

Do animals dream?

Yes, animals dream while they sleep, and you can often tell when that happens if you watch them. Dogs, for example, will twitch and perk up their ears as if they were listening to something only they can hear. They growl and move their legs as if they were trying to go somewhere. Other animals go through these body motions in their sleep, too. Watch closely next time your pet falls asleep.

Why do you cough?

When there is something blocking the air you breathe from getting to your lungs, it's your body's job to get rid of it. You cough to push air through your windpipe so that the irritating thing will get pushed out. Then you can breathe freely again.

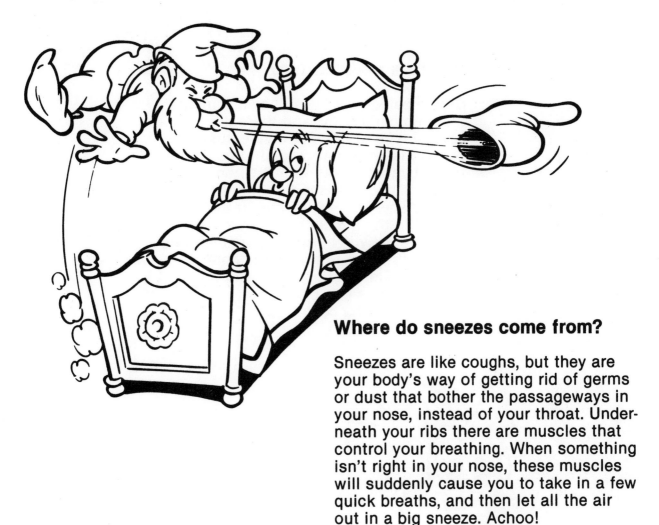

Where do sneezes come from?

Sneezes are like coughs, but they are your body's way of getting rid of germs or dust that bother the passageways in your nose, instead of your throat. Underneath your ribs there are muscles that control your breathing. When something isn't right in your nose, these muscles will suddenly cause you to take in a few quick breaths, and then let all the air out in a big sneeze. Achoo!

Where do burps come from?

Burps come from your stomach, and they happen when there is too much gas inside it. Air is gas, and whenever you eat or drink too fast, you gulp down air at the same time. Soda, or anything that is carbonated (or has "the fizzies"), also brings air into your stomach. When you burp, you get rid of the gas by pushing it out again. Your stomach then feels better.

What's a belly button?

Before babies are born, they live inside their mother's body, and there is a special type of cord, or connecting tube, called the umbilical cord, that connects the baby to its mother. Food from the mother's body passes through the cord to the baby. The baby's end of the cord is right in the middle of its stomach. After the baby is born, it will eat with its mouth, so it doesn't need the cord anymore. The doctor cuts it and ties it up as small as can be. All that's left is what we call the belly button, or navel. Everybody has one.

What is the Adam's apple?

The Adam's apple is actually the place in your neck where your larynx, or voice box, is. Your Adam's apple moves up and down when you swallow or speak. When we are very young and just learning to speak, we are learning how to control the muscles in the larynx to make the different sounds of speech.

Why do some people wear glasses?

Everybody's eyes are different, and some people see better than
others. Wearing glasses helps the people whose eyes aren't as
good to see better. Some people can see well when things are
far away, but they can't see as well close up. They are what we call
"far-sighted," and their glasses allow them to see objects nearby.
Other people need the opposite help—they are "near-sighted"
and can only see things that are close. Their glasses make
faraway sights clear. Contact lenses make the same changes for
eyes as glasses, but they are worn right on the eyeballs instead
of on the nose!

Why do you get fat if you eat too much?

If you eat more food than your body needs for fuel to do its daily
chores, the extra food gets stored up as fat. If you do need the
extra fuel, your body knows how to turn the fat into energy.
Everyone has a certain amount of fat for the times it is needed.
But some people have more fat than they will ever be able to use.
If you get too fat, you can lose the extra fat by carefully
controlling what you eat so your body gets just the right amount
of food—and not a bit more. Then, if you need energy, and
you will if you exercise, your body will use up the fat it has stored.

WHAT IS MICKEY MOUSE MADE OF?

What is a film cartoon?

A film cartoon is a series of hand-drawn pictures placed together one-right-after-another and shown quickly so that the characters look as if they are actually moving. The word *animate* means "to bring to life," so a film cartoon is an animated film. It transforms characters from pictures on paper to life on film.

What was the first film cartoon?

Many thousands of years ago in a cave someone painted a picture of a wild boar with many pairs of legs going in different directions, trying to show that the animal was running. Then in 1736 a Dutch scientist named Pieter van Moosenbroek drew a series of pictures of a windmill with its arms in different places in each picture. He put the pictures on a machine that turned them on a wheel, and it showed the arms of the windmill turning.

When was Mickey Mouse born?

In late 1928, Mickey Mouse was created by Walt Disney and began his film career in a New York City movie theater. He opened in a talking cartoon (one that had sound along with the moving pictures) called *Steamboat Willie.*

Are the characters in a movie behind the screen?

No. When the movie is being made, the actors and actresses do get together to act out the scenes. A cameraman takes pictures with a movie camera. Then a movie director and sometimes the film editor go through all the pictures and put them together in the right order. When the film is just the way they want it to look, they are ready to send it to the movie theaters where you may see it on the screen.

Where do the voices come from in movies?

The voices of the actors and actresses, and all the other sounds you hear, are recorded when the movie is being filmed. The sound is recorded on a special type of film similar to the action film, and the two films are joined together so the timing is perfect—everyone's mouth movements match what they say. The machine that projects the picture from the film onto the screen also sends sound from the film into the air so that you can hear it.

Where are the people on TV?

Some TV shows are "live" and some are recorded. During a live show, the actors and actresses are in the television studio performing at the same time you are at home watching. Other shows, like TV movies or special shows filmed "on location" outside the studio, are filmed beforehand and shown later.

How does a TV work?

TV studios have special cameras and equipment that take pictures, turn them into electronic signals, and send them out into the air in waves that are invisible but very powerful. The antenna outside your house picks up such signals and brings them into your TV set to be changed back into picture form. This all happens very fast—as fast as light can travel—so that the picture seems to be coming from right inside the TV tube.

Can you watch the same TV show in Maine as you can in California at the same time? What about in London, England?

Because the signals sent out from a TV station travel at the speed of light, they can reach all over at almost the exact same time. To pick up a television show in London that is being shown in the United States, the signal must be strengthened on its way over to Europe, or it would be too weak to show up well when it got there. What we do is to "beam" the signal up to a communications satellite—a power station that is in orbit around the earth. There the signal is given an extra boost and sent down again in the right direction to London, or wherever it is being shown.

Where are the voices on radio coming from?

The voices you hear coming from your radio are coming from the radio station where a microphone does the same thing that the camera in a TV station does, but with sound instead of pictures. It changes sound into electromagnetic waves that are sent out into the air. Your radio antenna picks up these waves and brings them into the radio where they are changed back into sound for you.

How can a radio work in the car if it's not plugged in?

There is something called a battery that stores up electrical energy and can be used as a substitite for house current. A car radio works by means of a battery. The signals in the air are still picked up by the radio's antenna, and the radio changes them back into sound so you can hear music or news wherever you go!